Made Perfect in Love, by Dr. Marlene Miles

Scripture reference translations are indicated.

Published by Freshwater Press,

United States of America

ISBN: 978-1-960150-05-9

Paperback Version

Table of Contents

Made Perfect in Love

Freshwater

Freshwater Press

United States of America

God Freely Gives

The Word of the Lord came to me today: God wants you to desire to be with Him, to be near Him **more** than you feel to ask Him for *stuff*. He wants you to crave to spend time with Him, to desire Him, and to have a natural affinity and a closeness to Him. He wants you to seek Him, spend time with Him and be in worship and *relationship* with Him.

When thou saidst seek ye my face,

my heart said to thee,

thy face Lord, I will seek.

Psalm 27:8

Because God wants us to seek Him, God freely *gives*. God gives because a person's gifts make room for them. We can learn that from God: a person's gifts make room for them. Many times, that is why a gift is pre-sented. The gift arrives before you do, garnering favor with the recipient so you will be well-received to their home, and/or event.

God certainly gifts us extravagantly. In the natural, He's given us a planet, oxygen, Earth, soil, food, sunshine, and rain, among many other gifts.

Moreover, God gives us spiritual gifts and those gifts, as we minister to others, are the Gifts of the Spirit, and they make room for even the unbeliever to believe in God. The spiritual gifts make room for God.

··· for to one is given the word of wisdom through
the Spirit, to another the word of knowledge
through the same Spirit, to another faith by the same
Spirit, to another gifts of healings by the same Spirit,
to another the working of miracles, to
another prophecy, to another discerning of spirits,
to another *different* kinds of tongues, to another the
interpretation of tongues.

1 Corinthians 12:8-10 NKJV

However, God wants you to **want** Him more than you *need* Him, more than the gifts, but it is for this reason that He freely gives, so you are not consumed with asking, pleading, and begging for daily bread, or daily natural necessities.

But shouldn't we be asking for *spiritual* things?

Like a parent who takes care of a child because they love their child, because they first loved that child, God supplies all your needs because He first loved you. He first knew you before the foundation of the world and loved you then. He *first* loved you and is now teaching **you** to love. He who first knows a thing, teaches a thing, teaches the next person. So, God is teaching you to love.

There is no fear in love;
but perfect love casteth out fear:
because fear hath torment.
He that feareth is not made perfect in love.
1 John 4:18 KJV

Wanting to spend time with God implies that **we** love Him. God has taken the fear of not having enough from us so that we can be able to love both Him, and also one another.

If we live in fear of not having things we need for life, for godliness, we cannot love fully. The fear of not having enough does not foster love. We can't live in constant competition with one another either; if we say we have love, but we are jealous; that is not love. If we treat our brother or sister poorly, then where is the love?

God Has All Sufficiency

I'm from a large family and I hate running out of anything. But God! God, supplying all our needs takes that fear away. With fear gone, we are free to love rather than fear or consume one another.

Fear puts us in survival mode. No one can grow or prosper their souls in survival mode.

God freely gives. He supplies all our needs according to His riches in Glory. God supplies our needs; He doesn't sell them to us. God freely gives. He gives us life and that more abundantly.

- **Every morning: Tender Mercies.**

- **Every day: Daily bread.**

He readily forgives. He purges us from iniquity.

He gave us His Son, Jesus. He gives us water in the desert —in our dry places. Showers of blessings. Daily loads us with benefits, such as: Healings, and Deliverance. God graciously brings us out of survival mode.

One of the ways God protects us is by freely giving us the things we need for life and godliness, so that we are not at the mercy of a cruel enemy who would trick, deceive, or even try to destroy us to get the things *necessary* for life .

God freely gives. Have you ever been around a person who *freely gives*? It's an amazing lesson in graciousness and it tests your own feelings of self-worth. Do you feel worthy enough to really receive from a giver? Some people can't even receive a compliment. Not judging; I used to be one of those people.

Balance is needed here; can you really receive without being too aggressive?

Without being a greedy *taker*, or a fearful hoarder?

You should not have lack in your daily life because God *freely gives*. You should not have natural or spiritual needs because God *freely gives to us!*

My God shall supply all of your needs,

according to His riches in glory.

Philippians 4:19

You accept blessings or reject them by your own words, thoughts, and deeds. If you don't feel you are worthy enough to receive blessings, you may reject gifts and blessings if your self-esteem needs improvement.

What blessings, you may ask?

Well, if you don't know what the promises of God are, you must first learn what they are. Hear what those blessings are. Then you must believe that those blessings exist, and that they are for you. Believe God. Believe in God. Believe and you shall receive.

Have faith. Faith comes by hearing. Have faith towards God. Meditate on it. Mutter it, say it over and over again. Hearing it grows your faith because faith comes by hearing. Faith comes by *continuously* hearing, by active, present tense hearing. Not just by having heard and declaring, *"Oh, I know that Scripture."* Sure, you do. Surely you know that Scripture verse, but the Word of God is alive. The very Scripture that you may claim to know, the one you learned in Sunday School when you were ten years old, today, that same Scripture will *speak* to you, minister to you differently, at a higher level today than it did when you were 10, with your 10-year-old understanding, with your 10-year-old spirit. The Word of God can speak to you differently today than it did yesterday. God has got it like that.

As a man thinks in his heart, so is he.

As a man thinks in his heart, so is he.

Proverbs 23:7

So, you are to guard your heart with all diligence for out of it flow the *issues of life*.

Proverbs 4:23

What gets into your heart? That which you hear. That which you hear, by faith. The words, concepts, and ideas that you hear with repetition. That's why we are told if you want someone to remember something tell them three times. Observe the average radio or TV commercial. Notice how they repeat things at least three times.

If you want someone to believe a lie, just keep repeating it. That's called propaganda. If it gets through your ears and eventually into your heart, beware! Because eventually whatever is in your heart you will end up saying.

You can have whatever you say.

For verily I say unto you, That whosoever shall say unto this mountain, Be thou removed, and be thou cast into the sea; and shall not doubt in his heart but shall believe that those things which he saith shall come to pass; he shall have whatsoever he saith. Mark 11:23

This is Bible. All Bible.

Do not be deceived into speaking negative things over yourself and your life. Angels of God are on the ready, waiting for you to speak the Word of God, waiting for you to give them directions, to give them assignments as it were. Angels are ready and waiting to make things happen *for* you in the Earth.

You, as one person, speaking in faith can put 1000 angels to flight. Angels to flight? Doing what? Making sure what you just said comes to pass. For this reason, never say anything you really don't want. Try your best to not even *think* about things you really **don't** want. Because angels are waiting to make it happen for you.

Beware of counterfeits. The enemy, the devil has angels too who are waiting to make things happen **to** you when you speak negative words over your life. One can put a thousand to flight; remember that.

Do not be deceived into speaking negative things or negative words by repeating clever sayings, street lingo, casual jargon, and the lyrics of so many songs. Just because words are set to a catchy tune, a beautiful melody, or to a jamming beat, doesn't mean you should say them or sing them with your powerful voice.

You are set in authority, your words are not foolish gibberish, your words are very powerful. You are not a plaything. Your words are very powerful. Don't we hate it when people in high authority speak foolishly? You're in Christ, right now, seated in high places. We all need to take our own advice.

However, I warn you again, angels are not authorized to change what you say to what you meant. They are not authorized to change what you said to what is best for you. They must obey *your* WORDS. Guard your heart. Guard your mouth. Guard your words.

It you believe the Word of God then you can receive what He is freely giving. *Be* as if you have it already, by using your faith.

But God, who is all sufficient is **more** than enough. He's always present. He's always here. He's always nearby. So, there is no lack in the Kingdom of God. You just decide by your beliefs, words, thoughts, and actions *if* you will receive all, or any of what God has for you. Our God is freely giving; therefore it's on us, we really need to know how to receive freely and graciously.

If you have too much pride to receive from God, then ask God to deliver you from pride; I've had to.

Having a need can sometimes imply that there's *not enough*. You can *need* if you don't have enough, or as a child, you can have need if the parent, the adult, the *principal* person in the relationship *doesn't have enough,* or is *not freely giving*. But God *freely gives,* and He is and has more than enough!

Need can imply that which is needed is not enough, or the giver has that which is needed, but it is being *withheld*. God gives freely. God has given us so much. God has given us a **place**, provision, position, authority, power, peace.

One of the ways God protects us is by *freely giving* to us so that we are not at the mercy of an evil enemy. So, we don't have to go to extremes to have our needs met. We don't have to go into desperation or beg for the things we need for life and godliness. In God, there is no lack. God supplies all our needs according to His riches in Glory. Extreme need can lead to desperation and desperation can lead to being manipulated or overtaken by the enemy.

God has also given us purpose, an expected end, and good successes.

Delight thyself also in the Lord and He shall give thee the desires of thy heart. Psalm 37:4

God freely gives. So, you don't steal from a person who is generous and giving in nature. Just ask them; they will give you almost anything, even the shirt off their back.

Tenderhearted, merciful *people treat you how they want to be treated:* at first. They trust easily and may give you the benefit of the doubt if there is any doubt. But if you don't reciprocate or treat them well, they either walk away or begin to treat you how you're treating them. God is tenderhearted toward us, but He will not always strive with us. It is not good to provoke God.

After a time, even the tenderhearted may start to mirror and deal with you as you deal with them. God, too, eventually will answer you according to your own heart.

The heart is deceitful above all things, and desperately wicked: who can know it? I the Lord search the heart, I try the reins, even to give every man according to his ways, and according to the fruit of his doings. Jeremiah 17:9-10

So, I challenge you now if you're not praying, then God's not listening. Not tithing and offering – where's your money? The Bank of God is **not** open to you. If you're not worshipping God, that could explain why people aren't noticing you and are not giving you *your props*. You are being dealt with according to your heart, that is, how you deal with people. This is hard for a carnally minded person to see, though. A spiritually minded person may see the connection and get the lesson.

The New Testament says that denying Jesus before men, causes one to be denied before the Angels of God (Luke 12:9). Denying God before men? Then Jesus says He will deny you before the Father. Matthew 10:33

According to Your Own Heart

God will answer you according to your own heart, even though He's giving freely. Our Father is not a God of hardships and constant tests, trials, tribulations; He *freely gives*, but it is according to your faith and *according to your own heart*. According to your words, according to your beliefs, according to what comes out of your own mouth.

Sometimes we don't have because we don't ask. Or we can be ignorant to know what to ask for.

Don't be too timid to ask; He says come boldly to the throne. But, in balance, do not be arrogant or prideful. God resists the proud. If we ask with bad motives, we may not receive anything. Or sometimes we block the things of God by our own ideas, actions, and words, that may be amiss. We must repent of that. Renounce that negative behavior. God freely gives all things that pertain to life and to godliness.

First Loved

The Word of the Lord came to me today and this chapter stems from that Word. God wants you to desire to be with Him and near Him more than you feel to ask Him for stuff. He wants you to crave Him, desire Him, have a natural affinity and a closeness for Him, seek Him, spend time with Him. He wants you to be in *relationship* with Him; and He wants to be in relationship with you.

What do we love about God? We love God's Spirit. He is all Spirit. He is divine and He is good, and He is infinite, and infinitely good to us. We love these things about God. We love how and that God loves us, and we love the Word of God because it is Spirit and life to us. And we love God because He first loved us.

> We love because he first loved us.
>
> 1 John 4:19 NIV

There are many different love languages. One of the love languages is giving. One of the ways that God shows us love is that He *first* loved us. He gave. God so loved the world that He gave; He gave His *only* begotten Son. Yes, God also fulfills all our natural needs in our living. He gives us all things for our lives and for godliness.

He supplies all things to us according to His riches in Glory and we know that God is rich, and He is in Glory. As a parent who takes care of a child because they love that child, because they *first* love that child when that child didn't even know how to love, or how to express love. God is like that towards us. He supplies all our needs because He *first* loves us.

He loved you first and He's teaching you to love. Remember, he who first knows a thing, teaches that thing. He who first knows a thing teaches the next person.

Two People in Covenant

Because of needing to teach and model love, is why two people in covenant are the ones who are supposed to be giving birth to children, so, they can model love to the child, in the home, and show the child what love looks like, what it feels like, what it sounds like. They can show the child how love is expressed, one to another. The parents are to *first* love each other so they can then share that love with their offspring.

God is Love. God is not *need.* We don't serve a broke or broke down God. There is no lack in the Kingdom; there is no lack in God.

The Lord is My Shepherd, I shall not want--, ***want here, means lack.***

Love is a whole different thing. Love is like a warm comforting cloak, or overcoat-- a *Thundershirt*, or a weighted blanket that calms you down and keeps you peaceful even if storms are raging outside. You feel safe in an environment of Love, in a loving home, a loving embrace, a loving relationship. You know that you are accepted, and you accept loved ones in a loving environment.

God wants us to want Him more than we need Him. So, He freely gives.

We need to be like God. We need to desire to be desired versus just **needed.** Need usually means you have more than the person who needs you. It may result in you being **used.** Does anyone want to feel used or be used by another person? You would want to be wanted, you want to be celebrated and not just tolerated.

The person who feels they must be needed has self-worth issues. Would you be willing to be *used* just to have the *appearance* of a relationship? I don't think so. I'm talking to men <u>and</u> women here. Would you really like to have a fake relationship just to **say** you have a relationship? Of course not.

Aren't you good *enough* to just be wanted, to just to be loved, and not only needed?

Needed implies that I need *things* you own or have, or that I need something you bring to the table. Whereas being wanted speaks to my wholeness. It implies even though I have all the *things and stuff* I need for life and godliness something is still missing and that something is not a natural something, it's a *spiritual* or supernatural something and it's you.

Need Or *You*

When someone says they <u>need</u> you and they are trying to create a relationship with you, and you accept that proposition, that means that you either have to, or you plan to use that person, or you are willing, yourself to be used.

To need and to only need speaks of a transaction. I *need you*, means I either have to, or *plan* to use you. And/or--, you're willing to *be used*.

To need and to *only need* speaks of a transaction. When people do things out of necessity because they have to, and they really may not want to, that sets up a series of unfortunate problems.

Conversely, if I need a gallon of milk from the store, I will buy it. Money for milk; transaction over. No relationship with the seller of the milk.

I need a tank of gas; I buy a tank of gas. None of us will stand around and *visit* with the gas pump, talking over old times and making new plans for the future. No, you just buy the gas and then keep it moving.

I want you means, "I desire you, and I want to, and I desire to spend time with you and make future plans with you." Perhaps I also want to add to you, add to your life, not take away from you, by taking away what I *need* from you.

What are we giving God? What are we adding to the "life" of God? Or are we just taking, taking, taking? Transactionally?

Worse is when someone needs you to <u>need</u> them. *Let Jesus help y'all with that.*

We serve a God who is more than enough, so we can never deplete Him; but should we suppose, we can just *use* Him, as if

He's a vending machine or a huge wallet in the sky?

God is more than enough. God gives us Love. Love cannot be and will not be withheld. You can't hide love because love is too big to hide. It is bigger than you are. It's bigger than I am. It's too big, too powerful to hide or control.

Before I go any further, I remind us all, that love is a power. By God loving us, God is essentially giving us **power**.

When someone gives you power there must really be some trust there! I read somewhere that love is giving someone the power to destroy you but believing that they won't.

Love is a power that singers, poets, writers, great thinkers, and lovers everywhere, from time immemorial know and write, sing, and talk about, all the time.

Love cannot be withheld, restrained, held back, or quenched. But at the same time love can constrain you and keep you from doing things you might otherwise do. Love covers a multitude of sins and love can inspire you to do things you might not otherwise do -, good things.

But God first loved us, because He did, but in effect His first loving us shows us how to love Him.

God is not evil; He does **not** say, *"Imma **make 'em need Me"**,* like a captor with a woman detained in a bunker. He didn't say, "I'm going to show 'em," like a slave master. God is not like that. If anything like that is happening in a "relationship", those are also clues that is not love.

When you are *forced* to so-call "love" someone, as in a hostage or captivity situation, there's going to be trickery, Tomfoolery, on at least one side, probably on both sides, where you're both just playing games with each other. If you're being coerced, tricked, that's not love. But you've got to have discernment, pray, and ask God to reveal the truth of your situation to you. If there is manipulation, intimidation, or domination; all of that is witchcraft.

All the above leads to hurt, resentment, bitterness, hatred. None of this is God, it is all works of the flesh. All works of the flesh chip away at your spirit and diminish your soul.

God is Spirit, not flesh. He doesn't operate by works of the flesh. But, even if you fake obeisance in a "relationship", in your mind/heart, you're only going through motions. You can only take it--, you can only fake it for so long. Really, in the back of your mind, you're hoping and/or planning to get out of there. Planning a breakup, moving out and if the other person won't readily let you go, you are probably planning an escape.

Until then you might be playing along to get along, but that will eventually take a toll on you. It can keep you from growing and progressing as a person. It can reduce you to a shadow of what you once were.

God is merciful. He is all powerful. He says, "I love them," showing us that He's not fearful or prideful, so He shows us first that He loves us. He first loves us, and then draws us with loving kindness, tender mercies, blessings, attention and then we sooner or later (hopefully sooner) will *want* to be with God, spend time with God. Love God.

God has declared and shown His love to us. Obviously, anyone who loves wants to be loved in return. God is looking for love reciprocated. *God is looking for* **relationship**. *God is looking for long-term, not temporary, not just for right now. God is relational.*

God is not looking for robots. He's looking for hearts. God is not looking for artificial; He's looking for real. God, like us, is not looking for temporary; He's looking for keeps. Love is forever.

Lust is not forever, it's temporary.

When you want relationship with a person, you honor 1 Corinthians 13, observing, and honoring that love is patient, kind, not envious, boastful, arrogant, or rude. Love does not insist on its own way. Love is not irritable, or resentful. Love does not rejoice in wrongdoing. Love rejoices in the truth. Love bears all things, believes all things, hopes all things. Love endures all things and love never ends. In a loving relationship you, and your significant person, your spouse, all people involved. You all can just be yourself because you're in an environment of love.

A Representative

In any situation , other than a loving relationship, there's defensiveness, *deference, pretend*, play acting, or a get-over mentality with manipulation and fear which are works of the flesh. This will not prosper your soul; it will not grow your spirit, and it will not foster *relationship*. It is works of the flesh and that is oppression.

In any scenario other than real love, in order to deal with the situation, you must send your *representative*, which is some version of your real self to get what you want or what you think you want from that situation. Some people send their *representative* to work. It's kind of funny that when you call a business and push a button to speak to a representative, you may really be speaking to a *representative* because the real person may not even be there. They have sent some version of themselves to work to just get along, and play along, doing the minimum of work to get that paycheck that they need or believe they want.

If you are not yourself, you cannot be made *perfect*. Perfect love casts out fear. We are made perfect in love. If you are not genuine, not true to yourself and truly yourself, you cannot grow, you cannot change, you cannot prosper. Your soul cannot increase, and you cannot be perfected in love.

You should not have to just be a shadow of yourself at home. Home should be where it's safe to just be yourself.

You should not have to be a version of yourself at church; you should be able to be your real self and feel accepted. You will *never* have to send a representative or try to pretend with God. And you never should. God is not mocked.

Survival Mode

By first loving us, God takes fear away by giving us all things that pertain to life and godliness. There is no fear in love because Love and fear cannot exist together. Love is the greatest but fear rivals because of the flesh. Love does not operate *in the flesh*.

All of our emotions cause physical reactions in our bodies which makes those situations very real to us. The flesh is now and the impact on the flesh makes things seem very real to humans. Those impacts can throw humans into survival mode, which drives many works of the flesh. Love does not operate by the flesh, but it does have an effect on the flesh.

(More on this in the Survival Mode series by this author. https://a.co/d/9iCx2PD)

There is no fear in love; but perfect love casteth out fear: because fear hath torment. He that feareth is **not made perfect in love.**
1 John 4:18 KJV

If you are in fear, you are in survival mode. If you are in survival mode, you cannot grow. You cannot be made perfect in love while in fear. Love does not operate in the flesh. It can be *expressed* in flesh, but it doesn't operate in the flesh.

Love is a power. God freely gives us love, which means that God gives us power. Love *works* the power gifts of the Spirit. The flesh is affected by the power gifts, but the gifts do not work by flesh they work by faith. Those power gifts are, the gift of faith, gifts of healings, and the working of miracles.

There are other powers mentioned in the Bible, the Power to Get Wealth, the Power to Heal, the Power of Love, the Power *to* Love, the Power of Grace, Mercy, the Power of Forgiveness.

If you can't love, you have *little power* or you are *powerless*--, except by your flesh, which is usually by violence. You can make things happen by violence in the Earth. If you don't have love, you can't operate the power gifts. If you just use your flesh, that's usually violence.

Love operates thru the *spirit* of man. A man whose *spirit* is not developed cannot flow in love. I'm talking about the real, *agape*, unconditional, God-kind of love here. Oh, a man says he can operate in love, maybe he can: He operates in what he knows to be love, what he thinks is love...

- Yes, what he **thinks** love is –
- what he heard it is,
- what he saw at home growing up,
- what he **didn't** see at home growing up,
- what his immature friends told him,
- what his last relationship taught him that Love is...or is not

Love flows from the Spirit of God -- to the spirit of man, to the soul, and then it can impact the flesh. God gave the love for us to Jesus, *and* God gives love that is deposited into our spirit man. Love is the greatest power. Love is the great operator of the power gifts. Works of the Spirit are, *love, joy peace, longsuffering, patience, gentleness, etc.*

The love that Jesus has for us was given to Him by the Father. God gives love and deposits it in your *spirit*.

Father, thank You for freely giving to us, thank You for first loving us. Thank You, for Your lovingkindness, Mercy, patience and for teaching us to live and to love. Thank You, for giving us parents, teachers, friends, and loved ones who continuously show us love---, the *agape* kind. And we want to be more like You. Make us more like You every day, in Jesus' Name. Amen.

Lust Versus Love

When thou said seek my face, my heart said unto thee, thy face, Lord will I seek.

Psalm 27:8

God wants us to seek His face, and not to lust for the power that He has or ask Him for *things and stuff* all the time. God has a lot of stuff; all the silver and the gold is His. He owns the cattle on a thousand hills. He even walks on streets of gold in glory. We are not to lust after those things. We are to love the Lord with all our soul and all of our heart and all of our mind.

He wants us to spend time with Him. Here on Earth, we can practice love in our people-to-people interactions. It's probably one of the main reasons that we are here. I suppose loving God is easier than loving people, but we are supposed to do both.

What do we love about God? We love God's Spirit because God is all Spirit. He is divine and He is good. God is infinite and He is infinitely good to us. We love how and that God loves us. We love the Word of God because it is Spirit, and it is life. And we love God because He first loved us, 1 John 4:19.

What do you *love* about any person? Do you love their spirit? We could and we should. Their soul? We could and we should. Their mind, their will, and their intellect--, which is their souls. We should love their words and their ideas, their smarts, their sense of humor. Yeah, their soul. We have to love more than a person's flesh, or we can miss the entire person.

I can say with confidence that the flesh is rotting day by day. The flesh is the only part of a person that can wear out. Their soul should be prospering, and their spirit should be getting stronger. But the flesh—you can exercise it, feed it, and give it lots of water to drink, but time takes a toll. Unless God.

We can love the spirit of a person. But we must love more than just their flesh, or we'll miss the entire person.

I've found him who my soul loveth.

Song of Solomon 3:4

When you love someone, really *love* someone -- You love their soul. You know them deeply; you learn their spirit. you care about them deeply. Your soul loves their soul.

Can you imagine a teenager or young adult obsessing over a guy –saying, "*Oh, he loves my soul! I've got to prosper my soul because he loves my soul. And I want him to love it even more.*" God is like that. God loves you and your soul and your spirit. Wouldn't that be refreshing in human-to-human relations, though? Wouldn't that be amazing, instead of obsessing over losing or gaining a few pounds? Instead of going crazy over what to wear over those few pounds on a date to entice another person with flesh and then later to wonder, why he or she didn't get the know the real person and why he or she doesn't *love* them?

Lust loves *things and stuff*. Lust "loves" flesh, it lusts after the flesh, of others. Lust operates through the flesh, and it craves more flesh. Even carnal Christians who profess Jesus but are sight-, image-, and flesh-driven.

Real love, real *agape* loves the spirit and the soul of another.

Just as God wants to be wanted more than needed, shouldn't you?

Do you want to be in a so-called relationship where the other person is not really spending quality time with you, but is constantly asking you for *stuff*? I bet God doesn't either.

Need Versus Want

I dated a guy who broke up with me because he said I was too strong. He said that I didn't <u>need</u> him. I thought **not** needing him was a higher attractant than *needing* him. I thought becoming a whole person, in Christ and then choosing, <u>wanting</u> to be in a relationship with a person was the goal. Isn't that a higher thing than only *needing* him?

Perhaps he wanted a partial person that *he* could make whole. God-complex, anyone? Yeah, he was right; I am too strong for that.

Now I can report that since then he's gone through a couple of marriages with women who <u>needed</u> him. They used him and then they left. He thought that needing him would make them stay. Well, it did. They stayed as long as they needed him; then when they didn't *need* him anymore, they left.

Do You Like My Soul?

Once I asked another suitor, *"Do you like my soul?"* I told him when he liked my soul we can talk further. Pretty bold, huh? Give God the glory. He said that seemed like a lot of work to get to know someone's soul.

Since then I've learned that when people have sex with one another they are giving the other access to their **soul**. So, if you don't like their soul, don't sleep with their body.

Being needed may be flattering in a sense, but it can be draining. Especially since people who *need* you, usually need one or two things. Once they get that one thing or those two things and they no longer *need* you, will they stay around? And, if they leave, they've left with your soul, or part of it.

Worrying if they will stay traumatizes you in ***survival mode***. There is no joy, growth, or prosperity in survival mode. Survival mode throws you back into fear. Now you're in fear and there is no fear in real *agape* love. If you're in fear, you cannot also be in love. We cannot be made perfect or made whole in survival mode.

But the person who ***wants*** you wants all of you and accepts you as you are, loves you as you are, craves your time and attention, invites you to grow, and wants to be with you. That person is *all in*, and is all about you, of course, in a balanced way. We are not talking about obsessive or co-dependent behaviors.

So that person who is sincerely all about ***you*** sounds like God. But I believe there is someone for everyone in this Earth, as well. I sincerely believe it.

Do You Love Me?

In any relationship, if love is there, you don't have to repeatedly ask the other person, *"Do you love me?"* You will feel the love. You will know the love. You will feel safe. You will feel accepted. You will feel good around that person and about that person. And you will know that love is not being withheld from you.

Love, properly expressed, is too powerful to be withheld from you. It will be expressed to you in that person's love language, or, to you in your *own* love language if that person is prospered emotionally and understands that you may have a different love language than they do, and they have made the effort to learn and love you and communicate to you in your own love language.

You don't need to be in a relationship with someone that you have to constantly ask, *Do you love me?* He or she will either tell and/or show you that they love you. Period.

I Love You

I love you to the hearer means exactly what the hearer *believes* that love is. And that is exactly why they will either stay or run away once those words are spoken to them. Love can only be based on what one *believes* love is.

To the average person, Love is what you:

- lived at home
- saw at home
- didn't see at home
- what your immature friends told you love was
- what you saw on TV or at the movies

- how your first boy or girlfriend treated you
- how your last boy or girlfriend or ex-wife or ex-husband treated you

Based on:

- What they lived at home growing up.
- What they didn't see at home.
- What their immature friends told them.
- What they saw on the TV or at the movies, or,
- What was already in their heart when (if) they were planning to use the word, *love* on you.

Sadly, everything that was called or believed to be love that they've seen in their lives may be wrong. Got to ask God. Refer to the Word of God. There are a lot of Scriptures on love. Find them. Read them. Study them.

Toxic people weaponize the word, love to gaslight, breadcrumb, control, manipulate, intimidate. Words like this may be spoken: *"No one else is going to love you."* Or *"No one else is going to love you as much as I do, or like I do."*

Not so!!! Or maybe it is so. Maybe someone else may love you **for real** and not in a controlling, manipulative way. Toxic people may try to withhold love, which is really not love. Or they may plan to love-bomb, which is also not love. Both of those are manipulations.

But one may feel that as long as the other person is using the word, *love* that they may really mean it--that they may mean what you think it means, based on your history and your idea of love. So, it's better to communicate with your person and it's best to ask God.

In a "relationship" if ***"I love you"*** is said first, by the non-manipulator, the manipulator may think *the control game* is being played on *him* because that's how he was planning to use it! When he feels the game that he was trying to play is over, and he can't win, he runs away. It's what any of us who don't know what real love is might do—run away.

Unless you've met God and unless you've let God change you, renew you, improve you, grow you and lead you to maturity.

Unless you've met God and spent time with Him and with His Word! Unless you've spent time in God's presence! Then you'll know what real love is because <u>God</u> <u>is</u> <u>Love</u>.

Love? Yes, love. You may ask, *"When does that start?"*

It already started because God **first** loved us!

Don't get this twisted; a church girl, a praying church girl is not a pushover, an idiot, or a wimp. A praying man is not to be fooled with, either. They are kind, forgiving people, but they are **<u>not</u>** stupid. When you meet a praying person, you may have just met the most powerful person you've ever met in the natural. A person who prays may be one of the nicest, most peaceful, most forgiving people on the face of this Earth.

The person who prays is communing with God. Praying is communing with God, and that activity develops **all** the Fruit of the Spirit. Developed Fruit of the Spirit makes people a joy to be around. It takes the Fruit of the Spirit so that people will be able to even stand being around you.

Yes, that praying person is seeking God's face. God gives that person knowledge, insight, and Wisdom. That forgiving, kind and patient church person who is moving in love could be the best friend you would ever hope to have. Love is built on friendship, honor, respect, and trust. You really can't trick a praying person, even though their patience may make you think that you can. Even though your behavior may be horrendous, that prayer warrior is praying for your very soul, at least for a season. Trust that.

If a man would learn how to *first love* as God, who first loves us because He wants us to want Him, more than we need Him. then that man would be more like God. There he'd be in a situation where there is love, and where there is love, you are free to be free.

Whom the Son sets free is free indeed. You are free to be yourself. And when you are yourself, you grow, prosper, and mature and become the **you** that God intended you to be.

You become perfected in love.

As we follow Christ, we all need to learn to first love. I remind you that if you want to be with a person, around a person, honor 1 Cor 13 – Love is:

- patient
- kind
- not envious, boastful, arrogant, rude
- does not insist on its own way
- not irritable or resentful
- does not rejoice in wrongdoing
- rejoices in the truth
- bears all things
- believes all things
- hopes all things
- endures all things
- Love never ends.

None of the Above

Lust is none of the above! Lust is a work of the flesh. Lust often blames, saying, "Look what you made me do!" Lust is a childish, immature work of the flesh that takes no responsibility for itself and does not believe in accountability. Lust is not patient. Lust wants it now.

Lust can pretend to be kind, but really, it's not - lust can turn on you as soon as its *"needs"* are met. Sometimes one and done.

Lust is envious and competitive. Lust is even envious of itself. Lust sees what it *has* and wants something else, even while holding on the something that it originally wanted. Lust wants what it has, what it sees, and everything else that it thinks it will see in the future.

Dissatisfaction is a part of lust. There is no peace in dissatisfaction. Dissatisfaction is a part of or brings on torment. Torment is wicked and there is no peace, no rest for the wicked. Being constantly worried, looking around for more, more, more, never happy with what he has or what he most recently had is a form of torment.

He Just Loves Women

Some of you have probably heard men say that they just love women. Wonder what kind of *love* they have for these women. What do they love about all these women? *Agape* love? Surely, they themselves don't believe that. What do these men really love about women? Their souls, their spirits? Their 25,000 words they speak each day, compared to the 2500 that men speak, in the same time period? Their emotionality? Do you "just love" women because they cry easily or are emotional? What is it that you "just love" about women? Their soul? Their spirit?

When you love someone, you really love their soul. Your soul loves their soul. I am not speaking of soul ties or inordinate affection here, but of genuine love. Not codependency because you can actually function independent of the person and independent of the relationship, even if you prefer to be with your beloved. As you are taking time to learn a person's soul when you really love them, you don't have time to go from person to person like you're a bumble bee, trying to cross pollinate something.

Lust is completely different; it sees and seeks after, drools after flesh—, more and more flesh, like a mindless zombie.

One may be attracted to or by the appearance of another, by their looks, et cetera, but love actually loves their soul. Physical attraction is real, but many times arranged marriages, blind dates can lead to deep and meaningful love relationships. A mature person of dignity, such as yourself want to be loved and not just lusted after. And, like God, you too, want to be wanted and not just and only needed.

The insecure and unprospered don't behave this way. They look for temporary people to fulfill their temporary desires. I can say temporary needs because they feel that this is a _need_. These opportunistic types also look for needy people, because emotionally needy people are easier to manipulate into fulfilling the manipulator's perceived physical _needs_.

Who Will Run Away?

Conversely, and correctly, God is looking for *relationships*, God is supplying needs, so His people are **not** needy. God doesn't want us to be needy to the point of desperation or manipulation by others. God knows there is evil in this world and one of the ways He loves and protects us is by supplying all our needs for life and for godliness. In this way, we enter into genuine relationships with people who authentically care for us, and not because we are self-serving or opportunistic.

God too, wants to be wanted. He is long term, and He is relational. If He is like this, then we should be like this. We should desire and deserve to be wanted and not just needed or needing to be needed.

In the average interpersonal relationship, who's going to be the first to say, *"I love you"*? And will the hearer run away after it's said?

When a person learns to *agape* then they can give *agape*. They can both give and receive the love of God. When one learns to receive and give the love of God, the torment will be over. Sleep will return. Health is restored and life is worth the living again because there is deliverance in this.

Comparatively, lust is arrogant and rude as it brags of its conquests and escapades. Lust brags of its transactions, especially if the "transactions" didn't cost them anything, in the natural. Perhaps we can mention that those transactions **cost** aplenty in the spirit, but that will be at another time, in another message and/or another book. But trust me, they cost something. The cost of sin is death. Death of something, could be joy, peace, finances, health, marriage, other relationships – it costs something. Transactional beings don't realize that costs are built into the sin; instead, they are blind to it, or are pleased to think they got more than the other person did from that "transaction." Okay, they got over. I said it. Ever really wonder where that term, 'got over' came from? *Anyhoo--*

- Lust, being impatient is irritable and after bad deeds are done is often resentful.
- Lust rejoices in and is proud of wrongdoing.
- Lust does not rejoice in the truth- often the mantra is Shh! Don't tell anyone!
- Lust does not bear, believe, hope, or endure ANYTHING. Here today, gone tomorrow. Wham Bam!
- Lust does not last – it crumbles, falls apart...

When speaking of the power gifts, love is the great operator, while lust thinks it is the **smooth operator**. It takes no power to move in lust. It is the lowest, base nature of a man. Even a cave man can do it.

Lust is not seeking the *face* of the person that they may be saying they love. The age-old question, *What color are my eyes?*, still holds merit. Lust cannot look in the face of a person and that is why lust runs away, immediately after the deal is done, or ultimately. And especially if the other party says, *"I love you."* Lust is outta there!

When you meet someone who loves you for you, but *you* **run away,** check yourself. Is there a problem with your self-esteem? Do you know your self-worth and value? Aren't you worth real love? Did you ever learn to love *yourself*? Did you ever see love modeled in your life, in your home?

Perhaps you don't want to be with *that* person (long term)? Oh, that appears to be a lust-I-want-it-now problem. Pray to God, there is deliverance for lust. All you have to do is ask in faith and resist the devil and he will flee from you.

If you were the aggressor: then why were you *toying* with that other person? If they were looking for a relationship while you were looking for situationship, why were you wasting their time?

Check yourself. Check your motives; check your ***game.*** God will deal with you for dealing treacherously with people, all people dishonestly –, and especially God's people.

Use your words, make things clear from the jump when you meet people or enter into "relationships." There are people in the world who just want to sin. If that's you, find those people. I'm not recommending sin to anyone, but cavort with those loose, also-transactional people. Mess around with those people and leave God's people alone!!!

Find others like you if you are a reprobate or a person with a seared conscience, if you are soulless, there are other likeminded, soulless out here looking for exactly what you're looking for. Perhaps, though one day, you both can get saved and delivered together!

Warning to God's people: the no-strings-attached, transactional people are out there. They want you to *need* them so they can manipulate you. Whereas relational people want you to want to be with them, permanently.

If you don't mean a person any good, stay away from them!!! If you need them, identify what you need from them and tell them from the jump that this is transactional. This is not God's best, because God is relational, but at least it's honest. Either person to person, or between you and God, transactional is not God's way in interpersonal relationships or one another ministry. Because God is relational rather than transactional, it's the reason why you can't easily negotiate "deals" with God, but He blesses you according to your **relationship** with Him.

In no way should we conflate this with times that we are sent to speak to, or meet with people one time or a few times, as God has sent us. I am not referring to ministry encounters; I am speaking of love and family relationships that should last a very long time, ideally forever.

Check yourself. Check your relationship with God, that is *if* you have a relationship with God. Perhaps you don't if you do not know how to be *relational* with people. If you are only a transactional person, you really need God. God is Love; *run to Him*, not away from Him. He is pure, unconditional, *agape* love. Ask God. If you are a scorch the Earth kind of person, then you need God.

God is relational; He wants you to want Him, and He has established the Kingdom for His Kingdom believers that all of our needs are met according to His riches in glory. We are free to be. Free to grow, free to seek His face, enter into His presence and bless His holy name.

Made Perfect in Love

When thou saidst, Seek ye my face; my heart said
unto thee, Thy face, LORD, will I seek.

Psalm 27:8 KJV

You just can't pop out of High School and into college and *know* how to love, if you haven't been taught, modeled, and shown how to love. What is love? There are four kinds of love:

- *Agape* – the God kind of love what this book is about.
- There is *eros,*
- *Philos*, brotherly love.
- *Storje* is the kind of love within families. Sometimes *storje* and *philos* are tied together to make it three kinds of love

instead of four, but when they are put together, it is still considered brotherly love or brotherly affection.

What man thinks is love is not love at all; sometimes it's only lust.

It's not love if someone wants to control the other person in the relationship. If the man or the woman wants to deprive the other to garner their obedience--, no that's not love. If one person wants to have more than the other person to lord themselves over the person who has less than, that's not love. If the aggressor just needs to be *needed* for control, that's not love.

Again, let Jesus help you with that.

If this person wants to keep the less-*than's* in captivity, bondage, servitude, in the kitchen, barefoot, pregnant, or in slavery. Nope, not love.

God is love and God doesn't do any of that because that's not love. You have less than God, and so do I, but we still love Him. That's because there's love. God has way more things, money, power than we do, but we are not jealous of God. Because there's love. We are not jealous of God because there's love.

Love and jealousy cannot coexist. Fear and love cannot co-exist.

So where is that love? Where is this love I keep talking about? When does it start?

Well, it already started because God *first* loved us. But if you consistently feel fear within a relationship, there's no love.

Or there is *not enough* love, or the love is not genuine. The person is not showing you love, or you're not feeling love from them then you may be worried. Worry is a result of fear, or it leads to fear.

> [18] There is no fear in love; but perfect love casteth out fear: because fear hath torment. He that feareth is not made perfect in love. [19] We love him, because he first loved us. 1Jn 4:18-19

But we are made perfect in love. We are perfected, we are completed, we are finished, in love. The Hebrew word for *blameless* means, *made perfect.* The Greek word for perfected means, *without blemish, finished, complete, having reached an end.* In English perfected means, *to become mature, fully grown mature, lacking nothing, whole, without defect, complete.*

In the Bible we are commanded to love our neighbors, love one another and Lord knows we already love ourselves, or at least we're supposed to. Love is a commandment for man If you're stressed or worried that a person may leave you. That's not love, that's fear.

- Will they accept me?
- Do they *like* me? What if they stop liking me?
- Do they like someone else better?
- Can't have friends because you're being monitored rigidly. That's not love.
- Can't have female friends if you're male, or you can't have male friends if you're a female. God's not like that; that's not love.

Can't call after a certain time of day or night? Everyone deserves boundaries but is this person hiding something? You can talk to God 24/7 -- any time day or night, and that's love.

Can't go to their house unless you call first. Yes, boundaries are acceptable, but where is the freedom to interact with the one you love and the one who says they love you? If this person is oddly not available at certain times or on certain days, especially holidays, that's not love.

If you don't know that you know there's love, then there's no love. Love wouldn't dare leave you guessing.

If there is no genuine Love, *there is no love*. If you're unsure--, there's no love. Real love will make sure that you're sure. Real love is relaxed, it's fun. It's not regimented, it's not legalized, it's just real. It's fun actually. It's not programmed.

Love is home. Love feels like home; it's the most natural thing in the world. It is where you feel and are safe. Love doesn't lead to worry, anxiety or negative stress. And if you don't feel comfortable or at home you're not in a space or environment of love, then you're not *home*.

Even if your relationship becomes boringly predictable, that's still safe. Who wants to be with someone who is so changeable and mercurial, flippant, and they are different every day? I don't think that's exciting, at least not in a good way.

Jesus is the same yesterday, today, forever, (Hebrews 13:8), that's what I call dependable, not boring. That is called, stable to me.

Don't Run

Too many people freak out with the word, love—maybe we should just say, I *agape* you. Do you *agape when you tell someone that you love them?* or is it something other than agape? Is it just lust? And if you know what love is and you know how to love when someone says, *I love you* to you, you won't run away. When you're made of the stuff that God is made of, when you are embracing the stuff that God has put in you, you will be seeking love and not running away from it.

If you don't know what love is and/or you don't know how to love when someone says, *I love you*, you may be the runner. If you know what love is and know how to love, you probably won't run away.

You learned love from your parents first, then family, then friends, then in interpersonal relationships and somewhere in there you met God! And God really brought it home for you; He taught you what love is and how to love.

And because you first learned it from your parents, that's the reason why God planned for two to be in covenant to have a baby, so you'd have two parents to model love and teach you, show you, how to love, simply because they first loved each other.

A child needs to not only see how to *agape* like his or her dad and also the female version of how to give and receive real love like his or her mom. The child needs to see male-to-female honor, love, and respect. A child should see female-to-male honor, respect, and agape love. A child needs to see that.

Love is complex.

A picture paints a thousand words.

Unless They've Met God

It could take a long time for a person to learn love, how to be loved, how to receive love, and how to give love. They need to learn that love is an action, it is not just a feeling.

Babies *need* adults to teach them how to love. But where are those babies once they *become* adults, themselves? So many empty nest parents may be wondering the same thing. They may be asking, *"Where **are** my children?"* You have to teach your children to not only need you, but also teach them to respect, love you, and honor you.

Just as they would God, you are not God, but you are a version, on Earth that they can see of someone who is in authority over them, who loves them--, someone who *first* loves them, and provides their needs to them.

And so goes relationships. When you're older, when they're adults, when your children are adults, you won't have to wonder, *"Where are my kids? Where are my children? Why don't they call? Why don't they come around? Why don't they check on me? Why don't they visit?"*

Ultimately, *"Why don't they love me? Why don't they express love to me?"*

I ask you, is it because they don't **need** you and perhaps it's because they don't have any *needs*? Thank God that they are adults now, educated, employed, self-sufficient, since that was your God-given assignment and goal after all.

But perhaps at home, and perhaps from you, they only learned to **_need_** you. And if you've taught your kids to only need you, then that's what they are living out in the world right now in their lives.

Unless they've met God on the way. If they've met God, they've learned how to love. But if they are living out the notion that parents are only to supply needs—that's it, that's what they will also teach their children, unless they've met God on the way. I mean your children and your children's children having met God.

Where Is the Love?

Love is deposited in the spirit of man by God. Then the decision is made to love. It is a choice of the will; it is not just a feeling. A person needs to see love as well as experience it.

As a parent, if you are regaling your child with *things and stuff* and making sure they are happy – make sure you are teaching them to love. Where is the love? First and foremost, make sure you model love for your child, your children. Yes, like God, meet all their needs, supply all their needs, but model love as you love your children.

Loading your kids up with *things and stuff* teaches your kids to be **transactional** rather than **relational**. Especially if you bribe your child with things and stuff for good grades, and for allowance. Just give your child--, supply them with the things that they need and teach them how to love, just like God does.

Does your child have the privilege of seeing his or her parents treat each other well? Respect one another? Honor one another? Does or did your child have that privilege? That's a hard question in the times in which we live.

Love is so important because God **is** love and when you show and model unconditional *agape* love in your home, you bless your children's childhood. You bless his or her life. God is love, so you bless their life by showing him or her--, God.

And as the divine is the thing that is loved in every loved one, when your child has real, unconditional love as a memory, this is what makes that child call home and want to come home, even as an adult.

Even as an adult with family of their own, this is the draw. God is the draw. Is God in your home? Is God in their home? The peace in that childhood home is the draw. Love is the draw. That is what will draw them back home. And even if the parents have moved from the childhood home, the parents have that love and that peace within them, and they take it wherever they go. That is the draw. That is what makes a child call. That is what makes a child come home for holidays, occasions, and weekends, for no particular reason at all.

I have never heard anyone say that there was too much love in their childhood home, so they are running away never to return. Nope. No one. Ever.

Do you know what empty nesters talk about to anyone who will listen? Their children. When they last saw them. What their children are doing. Where they are living. Where they went to college or if they are stationed somewhere in the Military. If they came home for the holidays--.

Children's children are the crown of old men, and the glory of children are their fathers.

Prov 17:6

When it's the holidays or either parent's birthday, and the children all come together, when they come home to honor their parents, that is the perfection. That is what completes the parent(s) who is being loved on again.

As love that was given in gestation, in birth, infancy, childhood, and teenagerhood is returned back to the parents, it's repaid in kind. When love is given, when it's given to you, that is perfection. That is completion. When what you have sown in your children is realized, that makes you feel whole and complete. Not that you were ever really depleted of love by loving your own children. You may have been deprived of energy, sleep, and maybe sometimes depleted of money, but hopefully never depleted of love. That's when you realize that the life that you sowed into your children was not in vain. It's when you see life and love looking right back at you. You see hope and where there is life, there is hope. It's when you realize that love, real love never dies because it's living in your children.

You can't hide love. And many waters can't quench love. (EWF and the Bible, respectively)

Many waters cannot quench love, neither can the floods drown it. If a man would give all of the substance of his house for love, it would utterly be condemned.

Song 8:7

And that's when you realize the power of love, the power *in* love. The love that sustained you all these years and decades. The love that lifted you up when you were down. The love that was the bridge that carried you across raging rivers of hard times. The love that bonded you all together. You realize the real power of love when you see your own children all grown up and loving God.

Especially when you see your *children's* children learning to love and loving love, it's then that you realize that you've taken something that God gave you and made it into something real. Something that pleases God. Something that will last into the ages, into eternity. It's then that you see love looking back at you. When your children are there with you because they **want** to be there.

No one is asking for anything; all their needs are met. No transactions are being made. They are simply there to be together with you and with family, and to be **relational**. They want to be there to honor parents and to love on family. They are there because they desire to spend time with you. That's perfection. That is the completion. That is being made perfect in love.

The Perfection

That which God sows will prosper in the way that He sends it. And to see a seed fully grown and accomplishing what it was sent here to accomplish is powerful and humbling. It is then that you realize that God freely gave you a gift that took all of those long days and nights, all of those years to show itself for what it really is. You realize that your children really learned what love is, which is the greatest and possibly the most important lesson that you could teach them. Ever.

You need to love, and you must love, and you must be in an environment of love because we are all made perfect in love. We are all made complete in love. And God is love.

We will know him because we will be like him. For now in this time of imperfection we see in a mirror dimly but when the time of perfection comes we will see reality face to face... by God.

1 Cor 13:12 AMP

We are to be seeking love, giving love, receiving love – real *agape* love. Drawn to it like moths to a flame, not running from it. The greatest of these is charity, which is translated, *love*. As stated in 1 Cor 13:13 three things will last forever, faith hope and love, and the greatest of these is **love**.

But we shall know Him because we will be like Him, and He will also know us because we've become like Him, and God is Love so he knows when and that you've mastered love. You've learned love when you want to be with Him; you want to be near Him and in relation and in proximity to Him more than anything else and certainly more than just because you have a need, or you want to beg God for *things and stuff*.

When God realizes that you know the true riches, the true value of love, the power of love and because you choose it rather than *things and stuff*, He knows that you won't abuse love or misuse it's power.

God just gives you *things and stuff* because, really if you're not mature, there is only so much damage you can do with things and stuff, so God rains on the just and the unjust alike.

But the true riches, the real power has to be learned and earned as you know and grow. Love is the greatest power, and it can never be defeated. It can never be quenched or cast down.

So, when you come to spend time with God without coaxing, urging, or without asking for anything, you've mastered **love**.

When you treat one another well, your neighbor, your brother, your sister—yourself, you've mastered love, you've embraced love. You've accepted Love. You've accepted God and you've accepted yourself.

Having been created in His image and likeness you're supposed to be like Him, and He is Love. And that--, this is the perfection that God intended all along. We shall know Him because we shall be like Him. And if we are already fearfully and wonderfully made in the image and likeness of God, then we are intended to be like Him in purpose, and Grace and anointing, then we need to be full of **Love**.

It's when God knows that you've finally realized who you are. When you know what love is and you run to it and not from it. That is the perfection. That is the completion.

Now, because of your relationship with God, great things--, greater things can be accomplished in the Earth, and God can pour anointing on you and into you.

I can do all things through Christ—the Christ anointing which strengthens me. Phil 4:13 NKJV

We can all do all things through Christ which strengthens us.

We are all made perfect in His Love.

Therefore, you shall be **perfect, just as your Father in heaven is perfect.** Matthew 5:48 KJV

Amen.

Christian books by this author

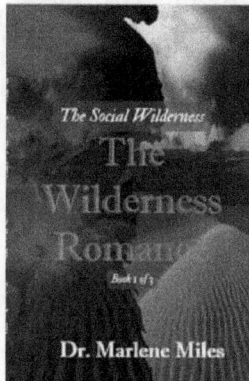

Many other titles by this author are available on amazon, Kindle and other platforms.

AK: Adventures of the Agape Kid

AMONG SOME THIEVES

As My Soul Prospers

Behave

Churchzilla (The Wanna-Be Bride of Christ)

The Coco-So-So Correct Show

Demons Hate Questions

Devil Weapons: *Anger, Unforgiveness & Bitterness*

Do Not Orphan Your Seed

Do Not Work for Money

Don't Refuse Me Lord

The FAT Demons

got Money?

Let Me Have a Dollar's Worth

Living for the NOW of God

Lord, Help My Debt

Lose My Location

Made Perfect In Love

The Man Safari *(Really, I'm Just Looking)*

Marriage Ed., *Rules of Engagement & Marriage*

The Motherboard: *Key to Soul Prosperity*

Name Your Seed

Plantation Souls

The Poor Attitudes of Money

Power Money: Nine Times the Tithe

The Power of Wealth

Seasons of Grief

Seasons of War

SOULS in Captivity

Soul Prosperity: Your Health & Your Wealth

The *spirit* of Poverty

The Throne of Grace, *Courtroom Prayers*

Time Is of the Essence

Triangular Powers (4 book series)

Warfare Prayer Against Poverty

When the Devourer is Rebuked

The Wilderness Romance

Other Journals & Devotionals by this author:

The Cool of the Day – Journal

got HEALING? Verses for Life

got HOPE? Verses for Life

got GRACE? Verses for Life

got JOY? Verses for Life

got PEACE? Verses for Life

got LOVE? Verses for Life

He Hears Us, Prayer Journal *4 colors*

I Have A Star, Dream Journal *kids, teen, adult*

I Have A Star, Guided Prayer Journal,

J'ai une Etoile, Journal des Reves

Let Her Dream, Dream Journal

Men Shall Dream, Dream Journal,

My Favorite Prayers (in 4 styles)

My Sowing Journal (in three different colors)

Tengo una Estrella, Diario de Sueños

Illustrated children's books by this author:

Big Dog (8-book series)

Do Not Say That to Me

Every Apple

Fluff the Clouds

I Love You All Over the World

Imma Dance

The Jump Rope

Kiss the Sun

The Masked Man

Not During a Pandemic

Push the Wind

Tangled Taffy

What If?

Wiggle, Wiggle; Giggle, Giggle

Worry About Yourself

You Did Not Say Goodbye to Me

www.ingramcontent.com/pod-product-compliance
Lightning Source LLC
LaVergne TN
LVHW051425080426
835508LV00022B/3251